Web3 and the Future of
Brand Loyalty

Navigating the Digital Revolution in Customer Engagement

Welcome to an explorative journey into how Web3 and NFTs are reshaping the landscape of brand loyalty and customer engagement.

1.
NFT &
Blockchain 101

The Evolutionary Leap: From Web2 to Web3

Introduction to Web2

Web2 marks the evolution of the internet from static web pages to dynamic platforms. It's where user interaction becomes a cornerstone, exemplified by the rise of social media, blogs, and e-commerce.

Key Features:

Centralized Data Control

In Web2, major companies like Google, Facebook, and Amazon dominate, collecting and controlling vast amounts of user data. Think of it as a few big libraries holding most of the world's books.

User Interaction

Here, the internet becomes a two-way street. Users don't just consume content; they create it, like writing their own chapters in an ever-growing book.

Business Model

The main revenue stream is advertising. Companies analyze user data to target ads more effectively, akin to tailoring a sales pitch to individual customers based on what they like.

The Evolutionary Leap: From Web2 to Web3 (Cont.)

Transition to Web3

Web3 is the next internet phase, embracing decentralization through technologies like blockchain. It's like moving from a few big libraries to a vast network of book clubs where everyone shares books equally.

Core Characteristics:

Decentralization

Instead of data being stored in one place, it's spread across a network, akin to distributing copies of a document across multiple locations for safety and privacy.

User Empowerment

Users have more control over their data, like owning a lockbox where they decide who gets access.

Interoperability

Different platforms and applications can work together seamlessly, like different book clubs sharing books without barriers.

Web3 Jargon and Core Components

Simplifying Key Web3 Components

Blockchain

Imagine a public ledger, but instead of being in one place, it's copied on many computers. Each transaction is a new entry, visible to all but nearly impossible to alter, ensuring transparency and security.

Cryptocurrencies

These are like digital money, but instead of being issued by a government, they're managed on a blockchain. They offer a new way of financial transactions that are fast and secure.

Non-Fungible Tokens (NFTs)

Think of them as unique digital certificates for owning things like art or music online, each with a unique identifier that can't be replicated.

Decentralized Applications (DApps)

These apps run on a network of computers rather than one central server, reducing the risk of downtime and increasing transparency.

Web3 Jargon and Core Components (Cont.)

Impact on Consumer Behavior and Expectations

Increased Demand for Privacy

- Web3 addresses data privacy concerns, offering users platforms where their data is respected and protected.

Authenticity and Transparency

- People now expect more honest interactions online, with a push for clear and open communication from brands.

Shift in Value Perception

- Users recognize their data's value and seek fair recognition for their contributions online, like being acknowledged for adding important information to a community database.

Implications for Brands and Loyalty Programs

Adaptation to New Consumer Expectations

- Brands must evolve, focusing on value creation through transparency, empowering users, and offering innovative experiences.

Innovative Opportunities

- Web3 enables new loyalty program models using blockchain and smart contracts, offering more **personalized and meaningful experiences** to consumers, like earning unique **digital rewards** that have real value.

2.
Why Web3 Loyalty

The Limitations of Traditional Loyalty Programs

Analyzing the Shortcomings of Conventional Brand Loyalty Strategies

Inherent Weaknesses

Limited Engagement

Traditional models often fail to create deep, meaningful customer engagement, leading to passive participation.

Lack of Personalization

Generic rewards systems lack customization, offering little personal relevance or value to diverse customer segments.

Data Privacy Concerns

Centralized data handling in traditional programs raises concerns about customer data security and privacy.

Changing Consumer Expectations

Shift in Preferences

Modern consumers, especially younger generations, seek more than transactional benefits. They prefer experiences, transparency, and a sense of community.

Statistical Insights

Studies indicate a decline in enrollment and engagement in traditional loyalty programs among newer generations, highlighting the need for evolution.

Traditional Loyalty Programs Defined

- **Basic Concept**: Traditional loyalty programs often hinge on point-based systems where customers accumulate rewards through purchases.

- **Transactional Focus**: These programs typically foster a transactional relationship rather than a genuine connection with customers.

Loyalty Programs

Need for Evolution

The evident limitations of traditional loyalty programs underscore the necessity for brands to innovate and adapt to changing consumer behaviors and expectations.

Understanding Brand Loyalty in Web3 Era

Reimagining Customer Engagement and Trust

Introduction to Brand Loyalty in Web3

- **Definition**: In the Web3 era, brand loyalty extends beyond traditional rewards, focusing on enhanced customer engagement and trust through the use of decentralized technologies. It's like moving from a one-size-fits-all rewards card to a tailored experience where each customer feels uniquely valued.

- **Shift in Loyalty Programs**: This section explains the transformation from standard point-based reward systems to dynamic and interactive models, powered by Web3. It's akin to evolving from collecting stamps for a free coffee to getting personalized rewards and experiences based on individual preferences.

Key Aspects of Web3 Influencing Brand Loyalty

Decentralization

Describes how spreading control across many participants (rather than a single company) can create a fairer and more transparent relationship between customers and brands. Think of it as a community garden where everyone has a say in how it's run, rather than a private garden owned by one person.

Data Ownership

Explains that customers managing their own data helps build trust and loyalty. It's like having a personal safe for your data, where you decide who gets the key.

Personalization and Exclusivity

Shows how Web3 allows for tailored experiences through technologies like NFTs (unique digital tokens) and smart contracts, offering one-of-a-kind rewards and access to loyal customers.

Web3 Technologies and Their Role in Loyalty Programs

Web3 leads to deeper, more meaningful interactions between brands and customers.

Technologies	Mechanisms

Technologies

Blockchain

Smart Contracts

Non-Fungible Tokens (NFTs)

Mechanisms

Token-Based Rewards

Customers collect digital tokens for their engagement or purchases. These tokens can also carry additional value in secondary markets, offering more than just brand-specific rewards.

Personalized Engagement

With smart contracts, rewards can be tailored to individual customer actions and preferences, making each interaction more relevant and engaging.

Exclusive Access and Experiences

Leveraging NFTs, brands can offer customers special access to events or products, deepening loyalty with the allure of exclusivity.

3. Real-World Brand Engagements Leveraging Web3

Real-World Brand Engagements Leveraging Web3

By incorporating Web3 technologies into their loyalty strategies, brands are creating more compelling and engaging customer experiences, as evidenced by initiatives from Nike and Starbucks. These developments showcase the potential of Web3 to revolutionize how companies foster and enhance brand loyalty.

Case Studies

FIAT Pass

Starbucks Odyssey

Honda Garage

FIAT's Web3 Transformation - "FIAT Pass"

Revolutionizing Automotive Loyalty with "FIAT Pass"

Strategy and Implementation

Launch of FIAT Pass

- Introduced as a dynamic, soulbound NFT program, offering unique experiences and real-world benefits.

Revenue Impact

- The program attracted over 55,000 participants, significantly expanding FIAT's customer engagement and data collection capabilities.

Key Features and Innovation

Dynamic and Soulbound NFTs

- These NFTs evolve over time based on user activity, deepening customer engagement with the brand.

Real-World Benefits

- The program provides tangible rewards such as mobility subscription discounts, access to special collectibles, and early car access.

Outcomes and Performance Metrics

Enhanced Customer Engagement

- The FIAT Pass program successfully engaged both new and existing customers, fostering a larger, more connected community.

Data-Driven Marketing

- Collecting customer data through NFT interactions offered FIAT richer insights for personalized marketing and product development.

Remarks:

1. **Company Overview**: FIAT, an iconic automotive brand, known for blending luxury with practicality.

2. **Project Objective**: To launch "FIAT Pass" as part of a Web3 strategy, aiming to redefine loyalty and ownership in the automotive sector.

FIAT's Web3 Transformation - "FIAT Pass"

Revolutionizing Automotive Loyalty with "FIAT Pass"

Key Insights and Lessons Learned

Web3 as a Tool for Customer Loyalty

- The success of FIAT Pass underlines the potential of Web3 technologies in creating more dynamic and engaging customer loyalty programs.

Community Building and Brand Loyalty

- FIAT's approach illustrates how community-centric initiatives can strengthen brand loyalty and attract new audiences.

Strategic Execution

Integration of Digital and Physical Worlds

- FIAT Pass bridges the gap between digital assets and physical car ownership, enhancing the customer experience.

Innovative Use of Blockchain Technology

- Employing soulbound and dynamic NFTs showcases FIAT's innovative approach in the automotive industry.

FIAT Pass NFT

The FIAT Pass case study exemplifies how an established automotive brand can **leverage Web3 technology to enhance customer loyalty and engagement**. By blending traditional automotive excellence with innovative digital solutions, FIAT not only **broadens its customer reach** but also **sets a new standard** in customer loyalty within the automotive industry.

Starbucks Odyssey – Elevating Customer Loyalty with Web3

Harnessing Web3 for Revolutionary Loyalty Experiences

Strategy and Implementation

Launch of Starbucks Odyssey

- In December 2022, Starbucks introduced Odyssey, a unique program within its existing loyalty framework, using digital stamps (NFTs) to unlock rewards and experiences.

Revenue Generation

- The program, with only 0.04% of Starbucks' 75 million rewards members participating, generated approximately $1,040,000 in its first year.

Key Features and Innovation

Gamified Customer Experience

- Odyssey engages customers through 'journeys', where completing activities earns them digital stamps, adding a gamified layer to the loyalty experience.

Exclusive and Diverse Rewards

- Participants can unlock a variety of rewards, from exclusive merchandise to unique experiences, enhancing the perceived value of being part of Starbucks' community.

Remarks:

1. **Company Overview**: Starbucks, a renowned global coffeehouse chain, known for its innovative approach to customer service and loyalty.

2. **Project Objective**: To launch a Web3-based loyalty program, "Starbucks Odyssey", aimed at deepening customer engagement and exploring new revenue streams.

Starbucks Odyssey – Elevating Customer Loyalty with Web3

Harnessing Web3 for Revolutionary Loyalty Experiences

Outcomes and Performance Metrics

Enhanced Customer Engagement

- Odyssey's introduction resulted in a 25% increase in regular app usage among its users.

Substantial Revenue Impact

- Despite its limited participant base, the program demonstrated a significant revenue impact, indicating a strong potential for growth when expanded.

Key Insights and Lessons Learned

Effective Use of Web3 in Loyalty Programs

- Starbucks' success with Odyssey illustrates how Web3 can be effectively used to revitalize and add new dimensions to loyalty programs.

Potential for Scalability

- The revenue generated from a small fraction of members highlights the scalability potential of such Web3 integrated programs.

Tips: Superfan Activation

- The Siren Collection sold out in 20 mins; 2000 pieces at $100 each.
- Initial sales yielded ~$800K from limited and open collections.
- Only 2.47% of stamps listed for sale; indicates high loyalty or low interest in selling.
- Secondary market value increased for most collections.
- Journey Stamps floor price averages $74; limited editions average $147, up from $100.

Starbucks Odyssey – Elevating Customer Loyalty with Web3

Harnessing Web3 for Revolutionary Loyalty Experiences

Strategic Execution

Focus and Simplicity

- Starbucks maintained simplicity in the program, aligning Web3 elements with its existing loyalty strategies.

Integration of Digital and Physical Experiences

- The program successfully combines digital NFTs with tangible rewards, enhancing customer engagement.

2023 Starbucks Odyssey Achievement Stamp NFT

The Starbucks Odyssey case study serves as an **exemplary model** for corporate leaders, especially in the **retail and consumer sectors**, looking to **innovate** in customer loyalty and **engagement using emerging technologies like Web3**. It demonstrates the **successful integration** of digital innovation into existing loyalty frameworks and highlights the significant potential for **revenue generation** and **customer engagement enhancement**.

Tips: Non-Web3 Native Focused

- Top 100 wallets hold $2.4M total.
- Average wealth per wallet: $24,292; median: $5,724.
- 54 ENS holders among top 100, surpassing many "OG" NFT collections.
- Indicates Starbucks Odyssey's appeal to both non-Web3 audiences and active Web3 collectors.

Honda's Web3 Evolution with "Garage NFT's"

Enhancing Global Brand Presence with "Honda Garage NFT's"

Strategy and Implementation

Launch of KEY NFTs

- Honda released "Honda Garage NFT's" aligned with events like the FORMULA 1 Honda & Red Bull Welcome Event and the F1 2023 Japanese Grand Prix, targeting global fans.

Total Mints and Engagement

- Around 65,000 GARAGE NFTs were minted, generating significant engagement through a raffle system for event tickets and Honda booth visitors.

Web3 Partnership

- Collaborated with Animoca Brands Japan and Gryfyn, indicating Honda's strategic commitment to the Web3 domain.

Key Features and Innovation

Cultural Connection via NFTs

- The Honda Garage NFT series aimed to bridge Japanese cultural elements with Honda's worldwide audience.

Metaverse Initiative

- Launch of "Hondaverse" in Fortnite, leveraging the game's 80 million Twitch followers to enhance brand visibility and engagement.

Remarks:

1. **Company Overview**: Honda, renowned for innovation in the automotive sector.

2. **Project Objective**: To rejuvenate brand engagement and counter declining sales through Web3 technologies, focusing on NFTs.

HONDA

Honda's Web3 Evolution with "Garage NFT's"

Enhancing Global Brand Presence with "Honda Garage NFT's"

Outcomes and Performance Metrics

Brand Engagement Uplift

- The NFT campaign and metaverse presence successfully elevated global attention and engagement.

Fresh Wallet Creation

- The initiative led to the creation of numerous fresh wallets, expanding Honda's reach in the digital asset space.

Partnership and Market Context

Role of Animoca Brands Japan

- This partnership emphasizes Honda's intent to merge Japanese content with global Web3 strategies.

NFT Market Dynamics

- Contrasting the success of NFTs in Japan with the Western market, Honda's strategy mirrors the regional acceptance and growth of NFTs.

Honda Garage Key NFT

Honda's venture into Web3, marked by the launch of Honda Garage NFT's and the Hondaverse, showcases a **novel approach in the automotive industry** to enhance global engagement. This case study exemplifies how **traditional industries can adopt emerging technologies like NFTs to rejuvenate brand presence** and **connect with new digital audiences**. Honda's strategy serves as an insightful model for global brands exploring innovative engagement methods in the evolving digital landscape.

Web3 and Brand Transformation: FIAT, Starbucks, and Honda

How did each brand uniquely utilize Web3 technologies to enhance customer engagement, loyalty, and drive revenue?

Comparative Insights

Engagement and Loyalty

All three brands leveraged Web3 to create more dynamic customer experiences, with each applying different strategies to enhance brand loyalty.

Revenue Opportunities

Starbucks provided clear revenue figures, while FIAT and Honda focused more on customer engagement and brand building, suggesting potential for revenue growth.

Diverse Approaches

Each brand showcased a unique approach to integrating Web3, from FIAT's focus on exclusive experiences to Starbucks' enhancement of an existing loyalty program, and Honda's cultural bridging through NFTs.

Strategic Takeaways

Digital and Physical Synergy

FIAT and Starbucks effectively combined digital innovations with physical experiences, while Honda used digital collectibles to enhance its global brand presence.

Adaptation to Market Trends

Honda's strategy was particularly influenced by the regional success and governmental support of NFTs in Japan, contrasting with FIAT and Starbucks' more global approach.

Community-Centric Models

All three brands emphasized the importance of building a community-centric approach, although their methods and execution varied.

The Web3 strategies of FIAT, Starbucks, and Honda offer diverse perspectives on how brands can leverage emerging technologies to evolve their customer engagement and loyalty programs. Each case study provides valuable insights for brands looking to explore Web3, showcasing the potential for:

Community Building

Innovative Engagement Strategies

Revenue Growth in A Digital-First Marketplace

4. Web3 Innovations: Transforming Brand Engagement

Web3 Impact on Brand Strategies: Key Insights for Pioneers

Streamlining Customer Engagement through Web3 Innovations

Opportunities to enrich brand loyalty and engagement

Blockchain for Trust and Transparency

Just as Samsung gained customer trust through transparency, blockchain brings this trust to your program. Customers see every transaction, ensuring honesty and strengthening relationships, just as it's crucial for market leaders.

Gamification and Wide-Ranging Rewards

Drawing from Starbucks's engaging approach, Web3 gamification revitalizes your loyalty program. It caters to tech-savvy consumers, ensuring your brand's relevance and appeal in a competitive market.

Efficient Development with Composable Tools

Reflecting the agility of brands like Grab, Web3's tools allow swift, cost-effective customization of your program. This adaptability is essential in today's fast-paced digital world.

Digital Ownership Enhances Brand Connection

Mirroring Fiat's deep customer relationships, digital ownership in your loyalty program fosters a stronger bond. This strategy transforms customers into active brand advocates and participants.

Web3 Impact on Brand Strategies:
Key Insights for Pioneers (Cont.)

Streamlining Customer Engagement through Web3 Innovations

Opportunities to enrich brand loyalty and engagement

Unique Rewards with NFT Integration

In line with the trend of digital collectibles, integrating NFTs offers unique rewards, setting your brand apart. This aligns with top brands' strategies of offering distinctive customer experiences.

Co-creation Strengthens Community Ties

Top brands thrive by building communities. Web3 enables co-creation, enhancing engagement and fostering a strong brand community, essential for long-term loyalty.

Interoperability

Echoing Nike's collaborative success, Web3's interoperability expands your reach and enhances customer experience, following the footsteps of top-performing brands. In an era where customer experience is key, as shown by top brands around the world, adopting Web3 with DOTTED is a strategic move towards a future-ready loyalty program.

Web3 technologies present a strategic avenue for Pioneers to **evolve traditional loyalty programs, offering enhanced security, engagement, and innovation.** This approach not only **deepens customer relationships** but also **positions brands at the forefront** of digital marketing trends.

Evolving Brand Loyalty for Today's Digital Natives

Integrating Web3 into Modern Loyalty Strategies

How can Web3 rejuvenate brand loyalty programs to resonate with today's digitally-native consumers (subtly focusing on younger demographics like Gen Z)?

Adapting to New Consumer Behaviors

Digital Natives' Preferences

- Today's consumers, particularly digital natives like Gen Z, exhibit a distinct penchant for immersive, digital experiences. They prioritize engagements that are not just transactional but are rooted in shared values and meaningful interactions.

Statistical Insights

- Statistical data paints a revealing picture of loyalty program engagement, showing a marked decline among younger audiences. This decline is a clear signal that traditional loyalty models are in need of innovation and transformation to remain relevant.

Web3's Role in Modern Loyalty Programs

Community-Centric Engagement

- Leveraging Web3 for creating community-driven loyalty experiences, aligning with the desire for meaningful brand interactions.

Exclusive Digital Rewards

- Using NFTs to offer personalized digital rewards, meeting the younger generation's interest in unique and digital-first experiences.

Evolving Brand Loyalty for Today's Digital Natives (Cont.)

Integrating Web3 into Modern Loyalty Strategies

How can this cutting-edge technology usher in a new era of brand-consumer relationships by seamlessly blending the digital realm with the world of loyalty?

Strategic Implementation

Recognizing Market Shifts

- Identifying the growing importance of digital and community-focused brand strategies to engage contemporary audiences.

Solution Integration

- Emphasizing the integration of Web3 technologies as a response to these evolving market dynamics, offering a pathway to enhanced customer loyalty and engagement.

In an era where **digital fluency** and **community values** are paramount, brands must evolve their loyalty strategies to stay relevant. Web3 offers a spectrum of tools for this transformation, providing opportunities for brands to create more engaging, **personalized, and community-oriented loyalty experiences**. This approach is essential for maintaining resonance with a generation that is reshaping **consumer-brand relationships**.

5. Start a Loyalty Renaissance with DOTTED

Shape Your Future with DOTTED

Your Pathway to Web3 Innovation in Customer Loyalty

dttd.io ↗

Contact us ↗

Capitalize on the Digital Shift

Embrace the Web3 revolution to redefine customer engagement and secure brand loyalty. With DOTTED, unlock the potential of blockchain, NFTs, and decentralized ecosystems to build a loyalty program that resonates with the digital age.

Strategic Insights for Your Brand

Learn from industry pacesetters—FIAT's exclusive experiences, Starbucks' gamified loyalty, and Honda's community-centric approach. DOTTED offers bespoke strategies to integrate these successful models into your business framework.

The DOTTED Difference

Our expertise in Web3 technology positions you to lead the market. Enhance transparency, empower customers, and offer exclusive, personalized rewards that set your brand apart.

Take Action Today

Connect with DOTTED to explore innovative loyalty solutions tailored for your brand's success in the dynamic Web3 ecosystem. Book your strategic session now and pioneer your brand's transformation.

Created by